You Can Read Music

Duane S. Crowther

Fourth Printing: January, 2005

International Standard Book Number:
0-88290-680-1

Horizon Publishers' Catalog and Order Number:
C2931

Combined English and Spanish Editions
International Standard Book Number:
0-88290-748-4

Horizon Publishers' Catalog and Order Number:
C2049

Printed and distributed
in the United States of America by

CEDAR FORT

Mailing Address:
925 North Main Street
Springville, Utah 84663

Local Phone: (801) 489-4084
Toll Free: 1 (800) 759-2665
FAX: (800)388-3727

E-mail: skybook@cedarfort.com
www.cedarfort.com

Contents

Introduction

Remember back in elementary school when you learned to read? Remember memorizing the ABCs, and then learning how to turn those letters into words? These words turned into exciting stories and wonderful new thoughts and great books about dinosaurs! Your new ability changed your life forever. You could read, and you discovered there were zillions of new ideas to learn and enjoy!!

Thousands—probably millions—of young people who are excellent book readers never learned to read music. You may be one of them. No one ever took time to teach you about the lines and notes you saw on printed music pages. How sad! You could have learned the techniques of music reading very easily, and had a lot of musical enjoyment that you've missed over the years. But now is the time to change all that. New opportunities and challenges await you!

Think of the wonderful sounds, feelings and ideas you can access once you learn music's alphabet and vocabulary. It won't be difficult. Now you can learn faster—you're more mature, and you're capable of absorbing new concepts at a much faster pace. And with this study guide, you'll find that you can learn the basics of reading music quickly and easily.

This book is divided into short lessons so teachers can present the concepts to you in brief, meaningful learning sessions and still have time for teaching their regular lessons. It is written with careful, clear explanations that can be easily understood. You can read it on your own and learn the key ideas, but what your teacher must provide, or what you must provide for yourself, is ***practice!*** *You'll need to look in your music and find examples of the ideas being taught. You'll need to practice naming the notes, and counting the measures, and identifying the ideas being communicated in key indicators like key signatures and time signatures.*

This book is precise in its presentations, but many key ideas have not been presented in full. Some explanations have been shortened and limited. Some related concepts have been omitted. You'll be able to explore those ideas later, after you've mastered the basic vocabulary and principles presented here.

But you can feel confident that when you've learned and mastered the ideas this book presents, you'll be very knowledgeable in the music-reading process, and your skills will rapidly improve. It won't take long. If you spend an hour on each lesson, and carefully memorize the few rules presented in word-for-word format, you'll find yourself musically literate in less than fifteen hours, and you'll say in retrospect that ***learning music reading truly was quick and easy!*** Good luck!

About the Author

Duane S. Crowther graduated with high honors from Brigham Young University with a composite major in choral and instrumental music education. He completed the course work for a Ph.D. in music education from the University of Utah. His doctoral dissertation formed the basis for the popular ***Teaching Choral Concepts*** curriculum which is widely used in secondary schools and in church and community choirs across the nation. He also earned an MA in Old and New Testament from BYU and an MBA from the University of Phoenix.

Mr. Crowther has taught music in the public schools, taught choral conducting on the college level, led and coached student stage and dance bands, and directed a variety of choral groups ranging from congregational choirs and barbershop choruses to large massed choirs and community choruses. As a music store owner and proprietor, he introduced hundreds of youths to their band and orchestra instruments, teaching each one personally to give all of them a solid start in music and performance fundamentals. He knows what basic knowledge is needed.

Throughout his adult life he has successfully combined his love of music, his love of teaching, his business interest and acumen, and his unique ability to write with clarity and precision to benefit many thousands of people. Truly, he's made the world a better place by sharing his talents with others.

1

Music Scores

This chapter provides a brief overview of how music is laid out in printed form. Many of the items identified here will be explained in more detail in later chapters.

Definitions: Score, Vocal, Choral

1.1 A **score** is a piece of music in which the performance instructions and parts are written out for the participants.

1.2 The term **vocal** means "uttered by the voice." In a musical context, it usually means an accompanied musical composition to be sung by a single individual.

1.3 The term **choral** means a musical composition to be sung by a chorus or choir.

Vocal Scores

1.4 A **vocal score** typically has a single voice-part line (called a **staff**) and two or more **staves** [plural of staff] for the accompanying instruments. If the accompanying instrument is to be a piano, the printed music usually will provide two staves, one for the pianist's right hand and the other for the pianist's left hand. This is an example of the beginning layout of a typical vocal score:

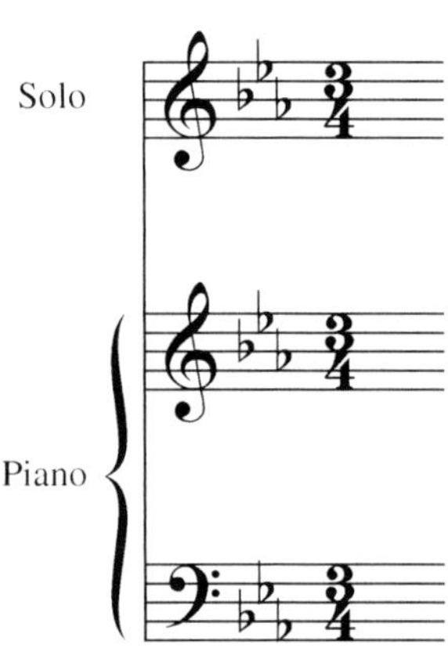

1.5 A **brace** is a connecting sign used to join two or more staves together. In the example on the preceding page, the piano staves are joined together with what music typesetters call a **piano brace.**

Choral Part Classifications

1.6 In choral singing, male and female voices are usually separated into **four main groups:**

A. **Sopranos** are *high female* voices.

B. **Altos** are *low female* voices.

C. **Tenors** are *high male* voices.

D. **Basses** are *low male* voices.

A choir which usually performs using these four parts is typically called a "**four-part mixed**" choir, or an "**SATB choir**" [standing for *Soprano, Alto, Tenor, Bass*].

Choral Scores

1.7 Hymnals and community songbooks often present their hymns and songs in **four-part music** on two staves, with any accompanying instruments playing all or some of the four parts. This is an example of a beginning layout for a four-part hymn arrangement:

1.8 In the above example, the **women's voices** would sing the two notes on the **top staff,** with *sopranos* singing the top notes and *altos* singing the bottom notes. The **men's voices** would sing the two notes on the **bottom staff,** with *tenors* singing the top notes and *basses* singing the bottom notes. Many choral music arrangements provide two staves for the singers, with two lines of music on each staff, so the choir is singing four parts in SATB style.

1.9 Other choral music arrangements, called **choral scores,** provide **a separate line for each of the four choral parts,** plus lines for the accompanying instruments. In the following example, the four choral parts each have their own part lines. There are two staves for the piano (identified with a piano brace), and two more lines for other accompanying instruments, in this case a string bass player and a drummer:

1.10 A **bracket** is a musical typesetting symbol used to group staffs together. In the example to the right, the four voice parts have been bracketed together.

Full and Condensed Scores

1.11 A **full score** for a choir, band or orchestra has a separate staff for each voice and instrument. It is also called an **open score.**

1.12 A **condensed score** is often made for combined choral and instrumental compositions in which all the choral staffs are shown, but *all the instrumental parts are condensed into a simplified accompaniment,* presented on the two staves of the piano accompanist's part.

Three Music Guidelines Begin Every Piece

1.13 **Three important music guidelines** are placed at the beginning of any musical composition, at the beginning of every staff. They are **always placed, from left to right, in the following order:**

A. a **Clef sign,**
B. a **Key signature,** and
C. a **Time signature.**

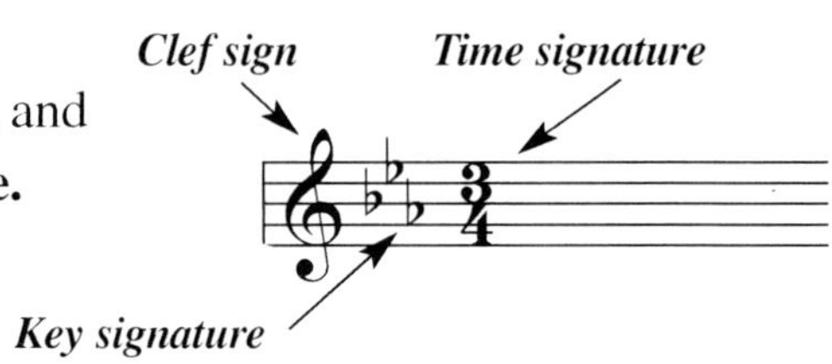

☛ ***Memorize the names of these important musical guidelines and their order, from left to right.***

1.14 A **clef sign** indicates the name of one of the five lines of a staff. There is a **G-clef** (treble clef), an **F-clef** (bass clef), a **C-clef** (that can be either an **alto clef** or a **tenor clef,** depending on which line it is placed), etc. The two most-used clefs are the **treble clef** and the **bass clef.**

1.15 A **key signature** indicates the basic tonality of the piece. Key signatures are expressed in **sharps** and **flats,** and can range from none to seven sharps or seven flats.

1.16 A **time signature** indicates the basic rhythmic accent pattern of the piece. It tells how many beats there will be in a measure and what kind of note gets one beat.

Rehearsal Marks

1.17 **Rehearsal marks** are letters, numbers, and other marks placed above the staff to help performers quickly locate specific points in the score. Several systems for rehearsal marks are used, including:

A. **Rehearsal letters:** letters placed above the scores at the beginning of musical sections, so the conductor can say, "Let's start at letter B."

B. **Measure numbers:** numbers are placed at the top or bottom of bar lines to indicate the number of the measure which begins at that bar line. These can be placed for every measure, or for some chosen interval such as every fourth or eighth measure, at the composer's or typesetter's discretion.

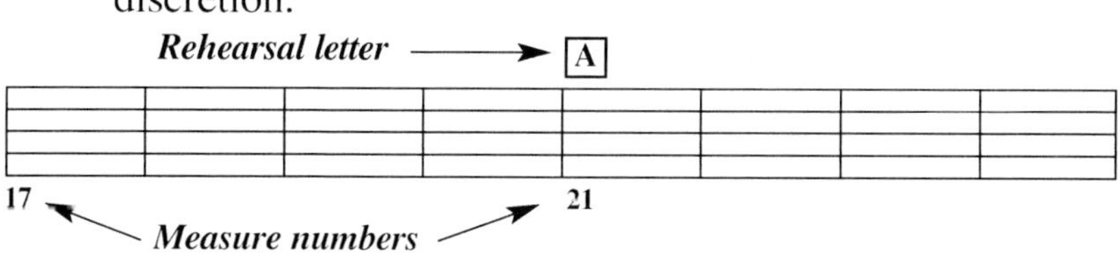

Chapter 1 Review

After studying this lesson you should know:

1. The definitions of the following terms: *score, vocal, choral, SATB, piano brace, bracket, full score,* and *condensed score.*
2. The four groups which perform in four-part mixed singing. Know which voice parts are sung by females, which parts are sung by males, which parts are high, and which parts are low.
3. Which note lines each of the four parts read and sing in four-part, two-stave music.
4. The three important music guidelines which are placed at the beginning of every musical composition, at the beginning of every staff.
5. The names of the three important musical guidelines and their order from left to right. Memorize them.

2

Measures, Bar Lines and Repeats

Definitions: Staff, Measure, Bar Lines

2.1 A **staff** is the structure upon which music is written. It consists of five lines separated by four spaces. [There are two plural forms for the word staff: **staffs** and **staves**.]

2.2 A **measure** is a grouping of beats on a staff. It is the space between two bar lines. Each measure contains the number of beats shown in the time signature.

Bar Lines

2.3 **Bar lines** are vertical lines drawn through a staff. They are used to separate measures.

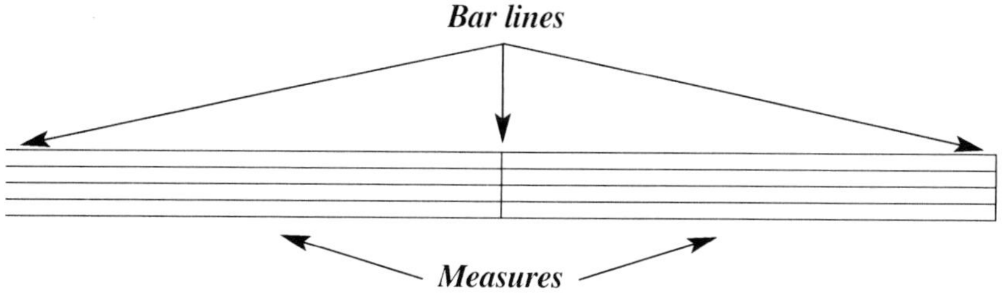

2.4 When **several staffs are bracketed together,** the bar lines extend through each staff, but they *don't* cross over into the white space between the staffs, since that is where the words to the song are written. However, the bar lines *do* extend through the white space of the piano accompaniment. This is shown in the following example, which includes four staffs [bracketed] for a choir and two staves [braced] for the piano accompaniment.

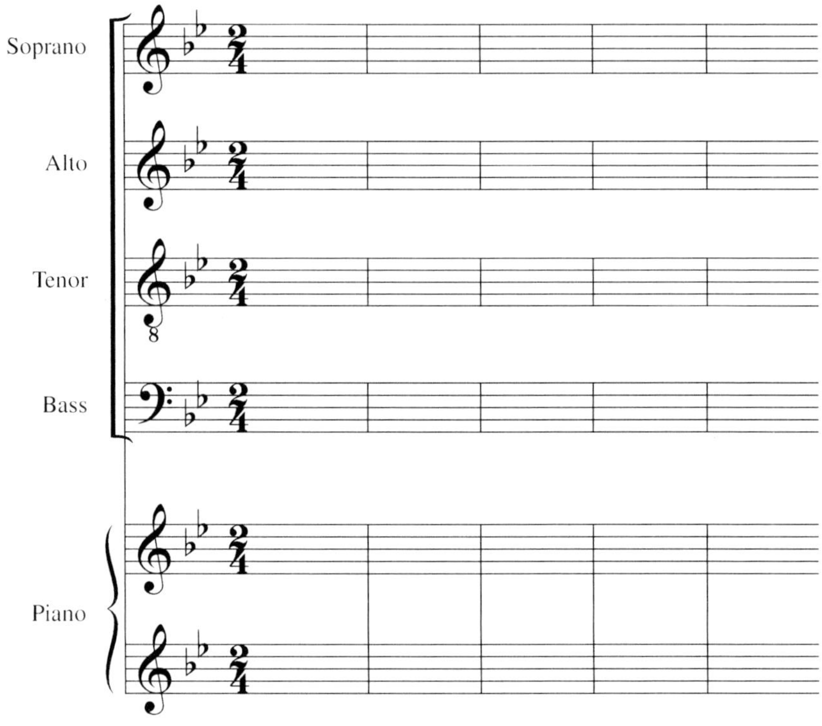

Double Bar Lines

2.5 Double bar lines are close-together vertical lines, drawn through a staff. They are used to signal

A. a **key change,**

or

B. a **meter change.**

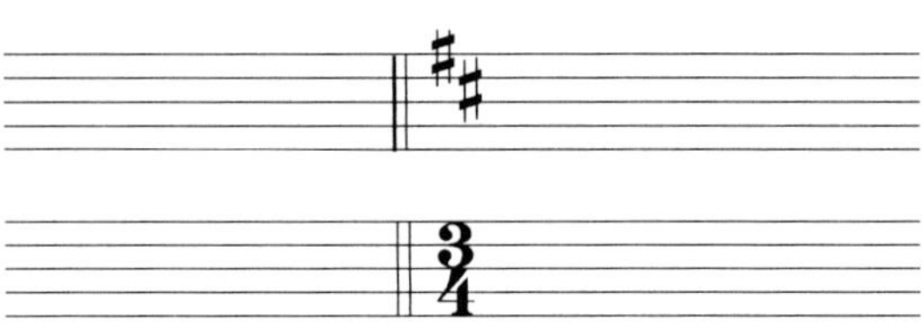

Section Dividers: Heavy Bar Lines

2.6 On some double bar lines, the left or right line is **thicker** than the other line. These thicker lines are called heavy bar lines.

A. When the *left line is thicker* than the right line, it signals the **beginning** of a section or piece.

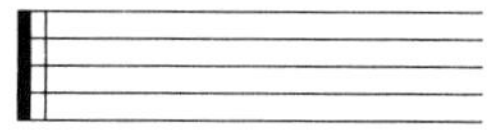

B. When the *right line is thicker* than the left line, but the *music continues,* it signals the **end of a musical section.**

C. When the *right line is thicker* than the left line, but comes *at the very end* of the music, it signals the **end of the piece.**

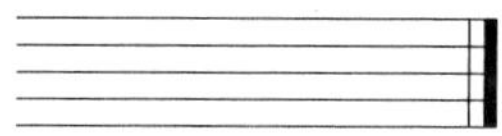

Repeat Signs: Heavy Bar Lines with Dots

2.7 **Double bar lines** with **dots** signal the beginning or end of sections that are to be repeated.

A. The **beginning** of a repeated section has *two dots facing right.* This is called a **begin repeat sign.**

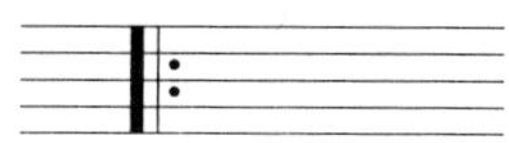

B. The **end** of a repeated section has *two dots facing left.* This is called a **repeat sign** or an **end repeat sign.**

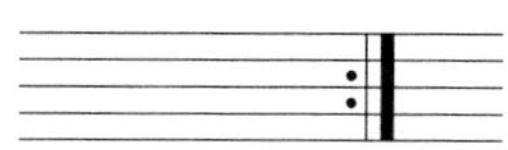

2.8 **Repeating music which precedes a repeat sign:** An end repeat sign, when there is no begin repeat sign, signals to go back to the beginning of the piece and again perform the music up to the ***end repeat sign:***

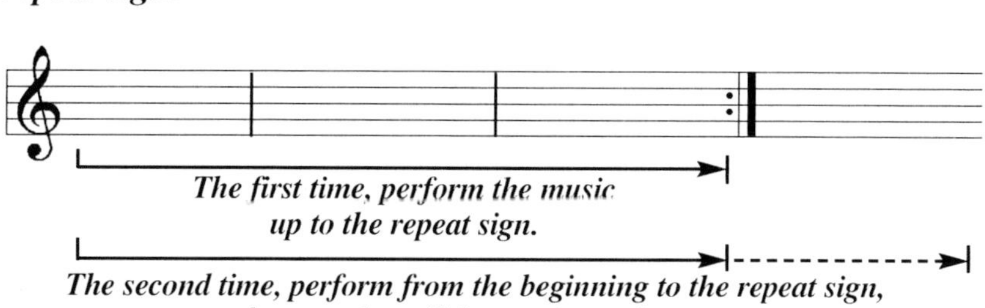

2.9 Repeating music between two repeat signs: The **end repeat sign** signals to go back to a beginning repeat sign and again perform the music between the two repeat signs:

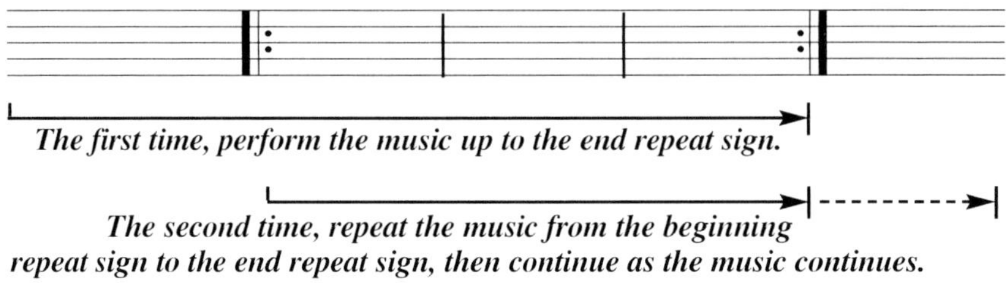

First and Second Endings

2.10 First-time and second-time bars are used in many repeat situations to change the ending notes of a repeated section.

A. The first time the music is performed, the section marked 1 is included. This section is called the **first ending.**

B. When the section to be repeated is performed for the second time, the section marked 1 is left out and the section marked 2 is performed instead. This section is called the **second ending.**

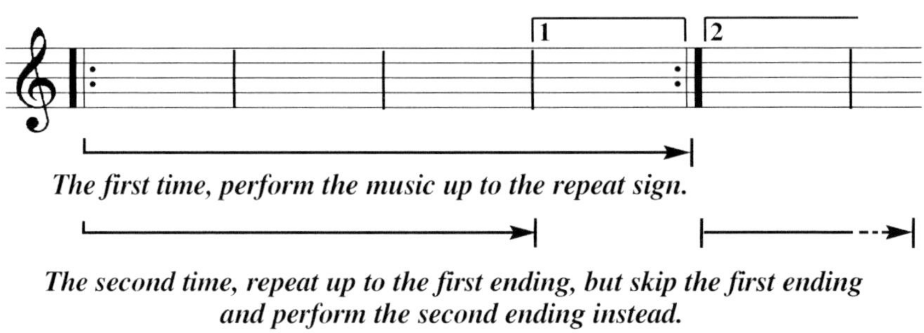

Da Capo: Repeat from the Beginning

2.11 The Italian term **Da Capo** [from the top] means *repeat from the beginning* of the piece. It is often abbreviated **D.C.**

Dal Segno: Repeat from the Sign

2.12 The Italian term **Dal Segno** [from the sign] means *repeat from the sign*. It is abbreviated **D.S.**

A. This is the **sign** used by music typesetters to show where the repeated section is to begin. It is placed above the staff for each part. 𝄋

B. **Dal Segno** means go back to the sign and repeat from there. It is placed above the staff for each part.

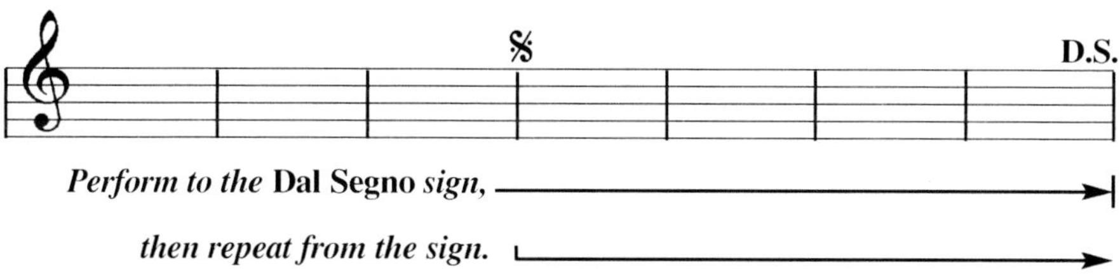

Dal Segno al Coda: Repeat from the Sign, then Jump to the Coda

2.13 The Italian term **Dal Segno al Coda** [from the sign, to the Coda] means *repeat beginning from the sign* 𝄋*, until you come to the* ***al Coda*** 𝄌 *indicator, then skip to the Coda sign* 𝄌, (which indicates the beginning of the final or **Coda section**) and perform to the end, which often is marked by the Italian word ***Fine*** [finish].

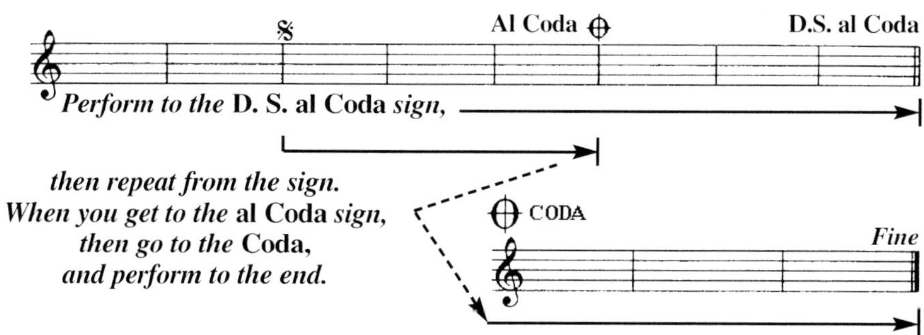

2.14 Know these terms:

A. ***D.S. al Coda*** - means repeat from the sign.

B. 𝄋 - The sign that tells where the repeated section begins.

C. ***al Coda*** 𝄌 - means jump forward from where these words appear to the beginning of the Coda.

D. 𝄌 or ***Coda*** - tells where the Coda begins.

E. ***Fine*** - means *finish*. It is usually written over a double bar to signal the end of the composition. The word is pronounced *fee-nay*, with the accent on the first syllable.

Chapter 2 Review

After studying this lesson you should:

1. Know the definitions of the following terms: *staff, measure, bar lines, double bar lines, heavy bar lines, heavy bar lines with dots, begin repeat sign, end repeat sign, first ending, second ending, Da Capo, Dal Segno, sign, al Coda, Coda,* and *fine.*
2. Know and be able to recognize how double bars are used: to indicate a *key change* or *meter change*, as the *beginning of a section, at the end of a section, at the end of the piece,* as a *beginning repeat sign,* and as an *end repeat sign.*
3. Understand how repeats are indicated: with *only an end repeat sign*, with *beginning and end repeat signs*, and with the use of *first-ending* and *second-ending bar markers.*
4. Know, be able to follow, and be able to explain *Da Capo, Dal Segno,* and *Dal Segno al Coda* repeat indicators.

3

The Treble Staff, Bass Staff, and Clefs

Note Names

3.1 **Musical notes,** and the sounds they represent, are named after the first seven letters of the alphabet:

A B C D E F G

After G, the note names begin again at A.

3.2 In musical notation, another note with the same name occurs every eight notes when notes are named from low to high, and from high to low. Two notes with the same names, eight notes apart, are called **octaves**.

3.3 In musical notation, the notes are laid out on **alternating lines and spaces.** If A is on a *line,* B is on a *space,* C is on a *line,* D is on a *space,* E is on a *line,* F is on a *space,* and G is on a *line.* But since there are only seven letters, the notes that were on a ***line*** in the previous group will be on a ***space*** when they're an octave higher or lower, and vice versa.

Evolution of the Grand Staff

3.4 **Music notation** has evolved since the Middle Ages. The number of lines in the staff has been changed several times. A four-line staff was used in the 12th century for a type of music called plainsong. Medieval notation sometimes used five-, six-, or seven-line staffs. *During the 15th Century, an eleven-line* **grand staff** *was used for a short time.* Musical clefs and five-line staves were fairly well established by about 1580.

3.5 The **grand staff,** also called the **great staff,** had eleven lines and ten spaces, with C as the name of the middle line:

Note Names

F
D
B
G
E
C
A
F
D
B
G

3.6 Because it was very difficult to read music written on eleven adjoining lines, musicians separated the grand staff into two staves, which came to be identified as the **treble staff** and the **bass staff.** In this system, which is used today, the line for middle C was omitted and the two staffs were spread apart vertically:

F
D
B
G
E

C *(This line was omitted when the eleven lines were separated.)*

A
F
D
B
G

3.7 **The imagined C line** is still the only line between the two five-line staffs, even though there is more distance between the top staff and the bottom staff in the present music notation system. When music is written which uses C, the note on that imagined line, it is written on a short line called a ledger line.

A. A ledger line *below* the *top staff* looks like this:

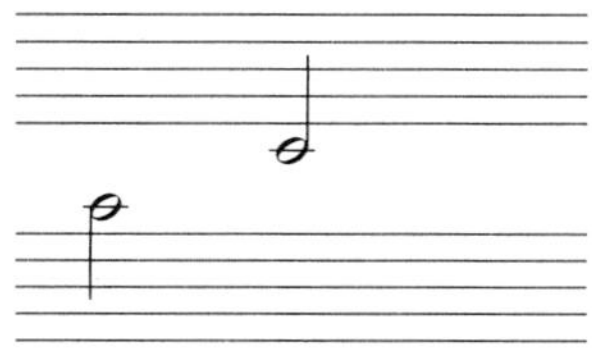

B. A ledger line *above* the *bottom staff* looks this this:

But both ledger lines shown above are indicating the same note, which is known as **Middle C.**

Middle C

3.8 **Middle C** is considered to be the **most important note in musical notation** because of its *central* and *pivotal* position.

A. It lies approximately in the **middle range of human voices.** Though it is near the high range of lower male voices, and near the low range of high female voices, sopranos, altos, tenors and basses all can sing it.

B. It lies **near the center of the piano keyboard.** It's usually the first note taught by piano teachers to their new students.

3.9 Since Middle C is **singable by all four voice parts,** the decision was made, centuries ago, to make a five-line staff above it which would *encompass the main singing range for female voices,* and to make a five-line staff below it which would *encompass the main singing range for male voices.* The *top* five-line staff was named the **treble staff.** The *bottom* five-line staff was named the **bass staff.**

3.10 Middle C is written on the staffs in these positions when various clefs are used:

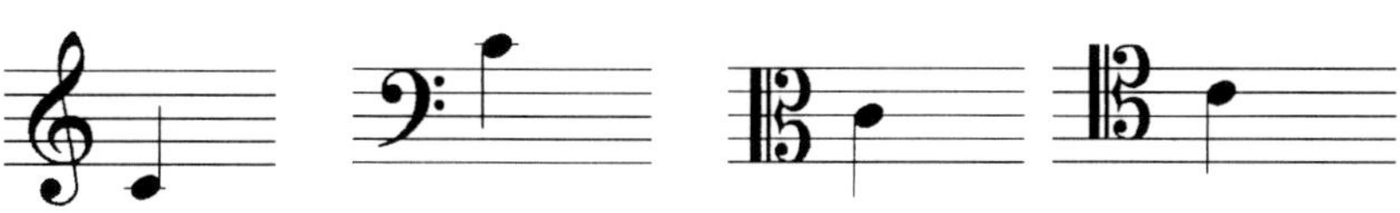

Treble Clef ***Bass Clef*** ***Alto Clef*** ***Tenor Clef***

The Treble Clef and Treble Staff

3.11 Clefs are symbols placed at the left of each staff which indicate the names and positions of the notes on that staff. They also help singers know which note line they are to follow.

3.12 The **treble clef** is used to write the music for high voices.

A. **All women's parts** (soprano and alto) are written in the treble clef.

B. The **tenor part** is usually written in the treble clef in a choral score, though the sounds the tenors produce are actually an octave lower than the written treble-clef notes. *Sometimes the treble clef is printed with an "8" below it to signify that the tenors are singing an octave below the actual written notes.*

C. The **treble clef** is used on **piano scores** to indicate the notes which are to be played by the right hand.

3.13 The treble clef is called a **G clef** because the circle in the bottom of the clef **"makes a bullseye" on the G line** of the staff (the second line from the bottom). The loop above the staff identifies the G an octave higher. The treble clef bullseye identifies the note G above middle C.

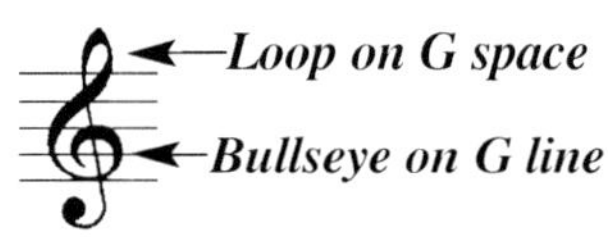

3.14 The **treble staff** is the **five-line staff** on which the treble clef (G clef) is positioned.

The Bass Clef and Bass Staff

3.15 The **bass clef** is used for **low men's voices: basses** and **baritones.** Many times music for **tenors** also is written in the bass clef. It is also used on piano scores to indicate the notes usually played by the left hand.

3.16 The bass clef is also called an **F clef** because the big dot is on the F line of the staff and the two dots on the right of the clef straddle the F line. The bass clef indicates the note F below middle C.

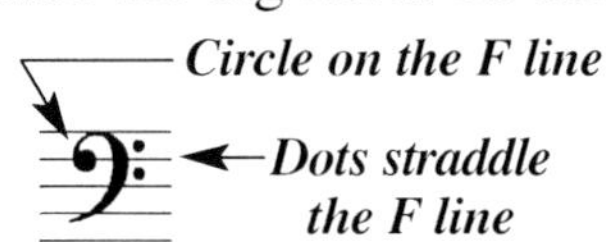

The Moveable C Clef

3.17 Occasionally a **C Clef** is encountered. Its use is quite rare today, but it is sometimes found in music written several centuries ago. It is called **moveable** because it can be placed on any line of a staff, with its "mouth" indicating the position of Middle C. Two moveable C clefs were most-often used:

A. The **Alto Clef** – places Middle C on the third line. Viola players often read this clef.

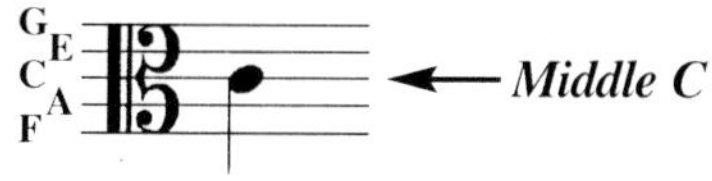

B. The **Tenor Clef** – places Middle C on the fourth line. Cello players often read this clef.

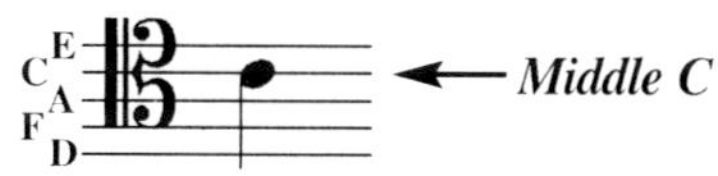

Chapter 3 Review

After studying this lesson you should know:

1. The names of the seven basic notes, how they are laid out on alternating lines and spaces, and why they alternate line- and space-positions when they are an octave higher or lower.
2. How the grand staff evolved and led to the creation of the modern treble and bass staffs with an imaginary line for Middle C. What the term **clef** means.
3. What makes Middle C significant.
4. How Middle C appears on the treble staff and bass staff, and when an alto clef or tenor clef is used.
5. How the treble clef identifies the G line and the bass clef identifies the F line.
6. What an *8* printed just below a treble clef means, and for which voice part it has meaning.

4

Rhythm, Meters and Time Signatures

Definitions: Rhythm, Beats, Measures

4.1 **Rhythm** is the organized motion of sounds in time. It consists of patterns of length and loudness which become musical designs.

4.2 **Beats** are pulses. Rhythms in most familiar music are based on a continuous series of identical pulses. These are equal length, low-level throbs or pulses that continue throughout the length of a piece.

4.3 **Measures** are short rhythmic units of equal length in which a set number of beats are grouped together. The most common measures contain 2, 3, 4, 6, or 9 beats. Measures are separated by vertical lines called **bar lines** (or measure lines), drawn through the staff.

Primary and Secondary Accents

4.4 **Meter** is the regular pattern of beats and accents found in each measure.

4.5 An **accent** is a note performed with a slight extra emphasis. Every measure has an accent on its *first* beat. It is called the measure's **primary accent.**

4.6 Measures with more than three beats have both a primary accent and one or more secondary accents.

A. *Measures containing four beats* have a **secondary accent** placed on the *third* beat of each measure.

B. *Measures containing six beats* have a **secondary accent** placed on the *fourth* beat of each measure.

C. *Measures containing nine beats* have **secondary accents** placed on the *fourth* and *seventh* beats of each measure.

What Time Signatures Mean

4.7 The **time signature** of a piece of music indicates the composition's meter—the basic pattern of its beats and accents. The time signature is placed on the staff immediately following the clef and key signature. A time signature consists of *two numbers, one above the other.* It looks like a fraction written without a dividing line, but it does not have the same meaning as a fraction in mathematics.

4.8 The **upper number of a time signature** tells how many beats there are in a measure. This is especially important.
☛ ***Memorize this sentence, word for word:***
The top number tells how many beats there are in a measure.

4.9 The **lower number of a time signature** indicates which note value has the pulse. This is especially important.
☛ ***Memorize this sentence, word for word:***
The bottom number tells what kind of note gets one beat.

Common Time Signatures

4.10 The most common time signatures are:

A. $\begin{smallmatrix}2\\4\end{smallmatrix}$ [*Spoken:* **two-four time**]
Two beats to a measure; a quarter note gets one beat.

B. $\begin{smallmatrix}3\\4\end{smallmatrix}$ [*Spoken:* **three-four time**]
Three beats to a measure; a quarter note gets one beat.

C. $\begin{smallmatrix}4\\4\end{smallmatrix}$ or **C** [*Spoken:* **four-four time,** or **common time**]
Four beats to a measure; a quarter note gets one beat.

D. ₵ [*Spoken:* **cut time**]
Two beats to a measure; two quarter notes get one beat. (The music is written with four quarter notes to the measure, but is played too fast to be directed in four, so it is directed with two beats to the measure.)

E. $\begin{smallmatrix}2\\2\end{smallmatrix}$ [*Spoken:* **two-two time**]
Two beats to a measure; a half-note gets one beat.

F. $\begin{smallmatrix}6\\8\end{smallmatrix}$ [*Spoken:* **six-eight time**]
Six beats to a measure; an eighth note gets one beat. *When fast:* Two beats to a measure; three eighth notes get one beat.

G. $\begin{smallmatrix}9\\8\end{smallmatrix}$ [*Spoken:* **nine-eight time**]
Nine beats to a measure; an eighth note gets one beat. *When fast:* Three beats to a measure; three eighth notes get one beat.

Basic Meters

4.11 The **three basic meters** are *duple* meter, *triple* meter, and *quadruple* meter. These terms tell how many beats per measure the conductor will use when conducting the piece.

4.12 **Duple meter** has *two* beats per measure. Typical duple meter time signatures are $\begin{smallmatrix}2\\2\end{smallmatrix}$, $\begin{smallmatrix}2\\4\end{smallmatrix}$ and ₵.

4.13 **Triple meter** has *three* beats per measure. The most common triple meter time signatures are $\begin{smallmatrix}3\\4\end{smallmatrix}$ and $\begin{smallmatrix}3\\8\end{smallmatrix}$.

4.14 **Quadruple meter** has *four* beats per measure. It is also called **common time.** Typical quadruple meter time signatures are $\begin{smallmatrix}4\\4\end{smallmatrix}$ and **C**.

4.15 Compound duple meter has *four* beats per measure, but is usually performed fast enough that the conductor only directs two beats per measure. This is called "cut time." This is the typical march tempo. The major accents are felt on the first and third beats. The most common time signature is ¢.

4.16 Compound triple meter has *nine* beats per measure, but is usually performed fast enough that the conductor only directs three beats per measure. The major accent is felt on the first beat. The most common time signature is $\frac{9}{8}$.

Basic Conducting Patterns

4.17 Music directors use different conducting patterns when leading music written in various meters. The following are examples of popular patterns, as seen by the performers:

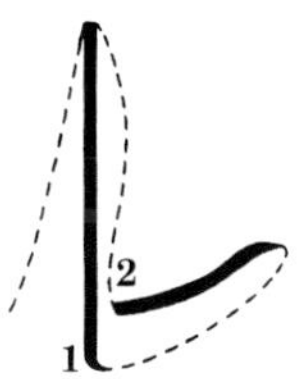

A. This pattern is used when leading music written in *duple meter*, usually $\frac{2}{2}$, $\frac{2}{4}$ and ¢.

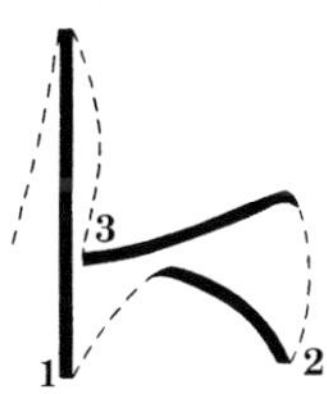

B. This pattern is used when leading music written in *triple meter*, usually $\frac{3}{4}$, $\frac{3}{8}$, and $\frac{9}{8}$ when it is fast enough to be divided in three beats per measure.

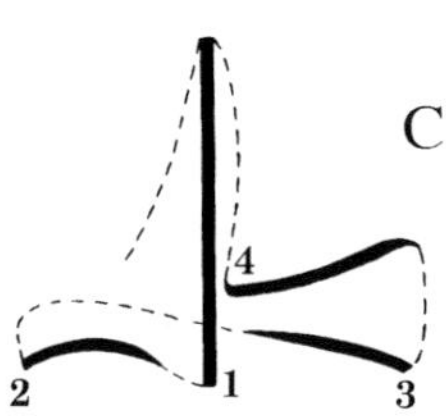

C. This pattern is used when leading music written in *quadruple meter*, usually $\frac{4}{4}$ and C.

D. This pattern is used when leading music written with six beats to the measure, such as $\frac{6}{8}$ or $\frac{6}{4}$. It would be used in slow tempos when all six beats are directed.

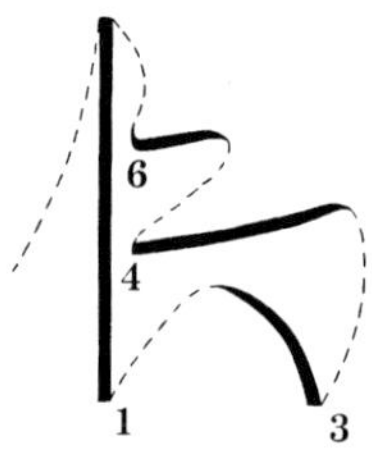

E. When the tempo is faster, $\frac{6}{8}$ is usually led with two beats per measure. When $\frac{6}{8}$ tempo is "inbetween" [too fast to direct in six, but too slow to direct in two], some conductors direct with an irregular beat pattern using four beats to the measure while omitting beats two and five.

Chapter 4 Review

After studying this chapter you should know:

1. The definitions of the following terms: *rhythm, beats, measures, meter, accent, primary accent, secondary accent, time signature, duple meter, triple meter, quadruple meter, compound duple meter,* and *compound triple meter.*
2. Where the primary and secondary accents occur in measures containing four, six and nine beats.
3. The meanings of the upper and lower numbers of a time signature, with the descriptive sentences memorized word for word.
4. The seven most common time signatures, and what they mean.
5. How to explain common time and cut time.
6. What the three basic meters are and how many beats each one has per measure.
7. What the two most common compound meters are.
8. The basic beat patterns conductors will typically use to direct all of the above meters and time signatures.

5

Notes and Rests

Notes

5.1 **Note shapes:** The shape of a note shows **how long it lasts**, **in relation to the other notes in the measure.** The shape of a note includes its **head, stem,** and **tails.**

5.2 A **whole note** is the note value from which other notes' values are calculated.

A. This is a whole note: 𝅝

B. It is described as a white note (or an open-head note) with no stem.

C. In 4/4 time, it gets four beats.

D. In a measure in 4/4 time, there can be only one whole note.

5.3 A **half note:**

A. This is a half note: 𝅗𝅥

B. It is described as a white note (or an open-head note) with a stem.

C. In 4/4, 3/4, and 2/4 time, it gets two beats.

D. In a measure in 4/4 time, there can be two half notes.

5.4 A **quarter note:**

A. This is a quarter note: ♩

B. It is described as a black note with a stem.

C. In 4/4, 3/4, and 2/4 time, it gets one beat.

D. In a measure in 4/4 time, there can be four quarter notes.

5.5 An **eighth note:**

A. This is an eighth note: 

B. It is described as a black note with a stem and one tail.

C. In 4/4, 3/4, 2/4, 6/8, and 9/8 time, it gets one-half a beat.

D. In a measure in 4/4 time, there can be eight eighth notes.

5.6 A **sixteenth note:**

A. This is a sixteenth note: 

B. It is described as a black note with a stem and two tails.

C. In 4/4, 3/4, and 2/4 time, it gets one-fourth of a beat. In 6/8 and 9/8 time, it gets one-half of a beat.

D. In a measure in 4/4 time, there can be sixteen sixteenth notes.

5.7 Thirty-second and **sixty-fourth notes:**

A. This is a thirty-second note:  A thirty-second note is a black note with a stem and three tails. In a measure in 4/4 time, there can be thirty-two thirty-second notes.

B. This is a sixty-fourth note:  A sixty-fourth note is a black note with a stem and four tails. In a measure in 4/4 time, there can be sixty-four sixty-fourth notes.

C. These notes are relatively rare.

5.8 More on **stems:**

A. Note stems can go **either up or down.** Their direction doesn't affect either the length or the pitch of a note.

B. When a note's stem goes **up**, it is on the *right side* of the note head. When a note's stem goes **down,** it is on the *left side* of the note head.

C. Stems usually go **down** when *the note head is above the third (middle) line* of the staff. Stems usually go **up** when *the note head is below the third line* of the staff. When the note head is *on the middle line,* the *stems can go either up or down.*

This rule often is ignored when there is an extended line of ascending or descending notes.

D. More than one note head can be placed on a stem. 

E. Note stems are usually about 3½ staff lines in height: 

5.9 Beams:

A. When there is a row of notes with tails, instead of writing out each tail, a solid line called a beam is used to connect the stems together. A separate beam is used for each flag that would be on the note stems. For example:

This:  Instead of: 

Counting within Measures

5.10 Measure-counting basics:

A. Measures in 4/4 time using whole notes, half notes and quarter notes, are usually counted **1 - 2 - 3 - 4.**

B. Measures in 4/4 time which also use eighth notes may be counted **1 - & - 2 - & - 3 - & - 4 - &.**

C. Counting **whole notes:**

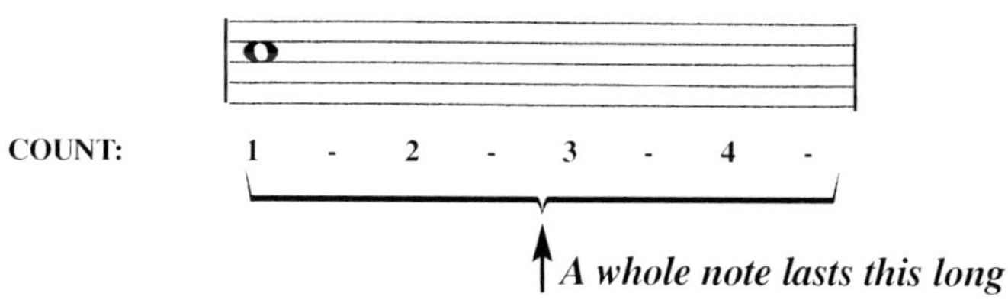

D. Counting **half notes:**

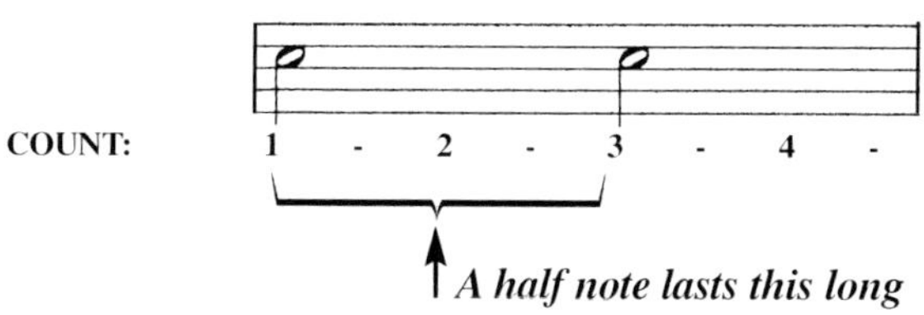

E. Counting **quarter notes:**

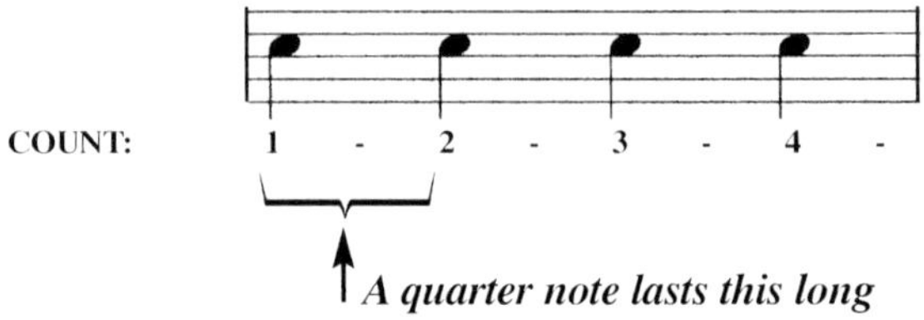

F. Counting **eighth notes:**

G. **Notes with different lengths** may be mixed together in a measure. The beat continues, regardless of the length or number of notes:

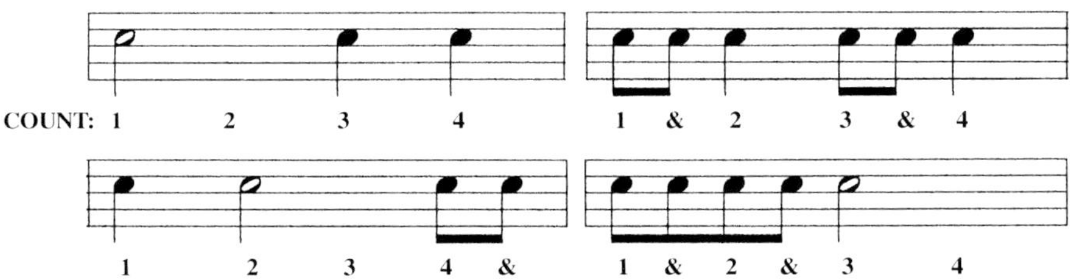

Rests

5.11 A **rest** indicates a *period of silence.* Rhythmic patterns often use silence as well as sound.

5.12 **Rest types** correspond to note types. There is a whole rest, a half rest, a quarter rest, an eighth rest, a sixteenth rest, etc.

5.13 A **whole rest**

A. A whole rest hangs below the fourth line of the staff, looking down:

B. In 4/4 time, a whole rest gets four beats.

C. In a measure in 4/4 time, there can be only one whole rest.

5.14 A **half rest**

A. A half rest sits on top of the third line of the staff, looking up:

B. In 4/4, 3/4, and 2/4 time, a half rest gets two beats.

C. In a measure in 4/4 time, there can be two half rests.

5.15 A **quarter rest**

A. A quarter rest stretches over the second to fourth lines of the staff and looks like this:

B. In 4/4, 3/4, and 2/4 time, a quarter rest gets one beat.

C. In a measure in 4/4 time, there can be four quarter rests.

5.16 An **eighth rest**

A. An eighth rest sits between the second and fourth lines of the staff and looks like this:

B. It is described as a slanted stem with an attached head extended to the left.

C. In 4/4, 3/4, 2/4, 6/8, and 9/8 time, an eighth rest gets one-half a beat.

D. In a measure in 4/4 time, there can be eight eighth rests.

5.17 A **sixteenth rest**

A. A sixteenth rest sits between the second and fourth lines of the staff and looks like this:

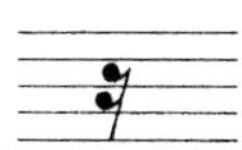

B. It is described as a slanted stem with two attached heads extended to the left.

C. In 4/4, 3/4, and 2/4 time, a sixteenth rest gets one-fourth of a beat. In 6/8 and 9/8 time, it gets one-half of a beat.

D. In a measure in 4/4 time, there can be sixteen sixteenth rests.

Counting: A Necessary Task of Musicianship

5.18 Learning to count music, and **disciplining oneself to count throughout the entire piece being performed,** is an *essential task* of good musicianship. Careful counting helps you *know exactly where you are* in the piece of music (thus eliminating that terrible "I'm lost" feeling). It helps you *know exactly when your part enters after long rests,* and exactly *when various notes begin and end.* It also helps you *hold tempos more exact* and *keeps you from skipping beats.*

5.19 Tips for careful counting:

A. Always watch and understand the **conductor's beat pattern.** Understand that the *down beat* always signals the beginning of a measure.

B. Remember the **meaning of the time signature:** the **top** number tells *how many beats there are* in a measure, the **bottom** number tells *what kind of note gets one beat.*

C. Learn to **count measures** as well as beats. For instance, count four measures of $\frac{2}{4}$ time this way: ***One,*** two; ***Two,*** two; ***Three,*** two; ***Four,*** two.

Chapter 5 Review

After studying this lesson you should know:

1. That note shapes indicate how long notes last in relation to the other notes in the measure. Note shapes give no indication of the tempo (speed) of the music.
2. The three parts of a note's shape.
3. How to recognize a *whole note, half note, quarter note, eighth note, sixteenth note, thirty-second note,* and a *sixty-fourth note.*
4. The rules for whether note stems go up or down.
5. How and when beams are used instead of tails.
6. How to count measures, using either quarter notes or eighth notes as the counting basis, and how long the various types of notes actually last in relation to the other notes in the measure.
7. How to recognize a *whole rest, half rest, quarter rest, eighth rest,* and a *sixteenth rest.*

6
Note Names, and the Names of Staff Lines and Spaces

Names of the Lines and Spaces

Learning the names of the lines and spaces in the treble and bass clefs is as essential to reading music as learning the names of the letters of the alphabet is to reading books. It's not difficult, and there are short phrases and words to help you remember them. ***The secret to learning to read music quickly is to thoroughly memorize these words and phrases and to repeatedly use them to identify the names of many of the musical notes you encounter.***

6.1 A **note** is a written symbol for a pitch.

6.2 **Seven note names** are assigned alphabetically from A to G in ascending pitches. The seven groups of A-G are repeated several times in music. (They are repeated almost seven-and-a-half times on a full piano keyboard.)

Low **A B C D E F G A B C D E F G A B C D E F G** *High*

The Treble Clef

6.3 The **names of the treble clef lines,** from *lowest to highest,* are: **E, G, B, D, F.** Notes written on those lines have those same names.

6.4 Two **often-used phrases** to remember the names of the treble clef lines, from *lowest to highest,* are: **Every Good Boy Does Fine,** and **Every Good Bird Does Fly**.

☛ ***Memorize both of them!***

6.5 The **names of the treble clef spaces,** from *lowest to highest,* are: **F, A, C, E.** Remember the word **FACE.** Notes written on those spaces have those same names:

The Bass Clef

6.6 The **names of the bass clef lines,** from *lowest to highest,* are: **G, B, D, F, A.** Notes written on those lines have those same names:

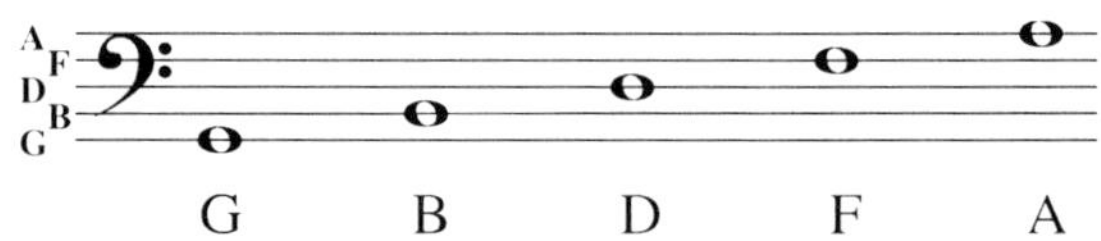

6.7 Two **often-used phrases** to remember the names of the bass clef lines, from lowest to highest, are: **Good Boys Do Fine Always,** and **Great Big Dogs Fight Apes.**

☛ ***Memorize both of them!***

6.8 The **names of the bass clef spaces,** from lowest to highest, are: **A, C, E, G.** Notes written on those spaces have those same names:

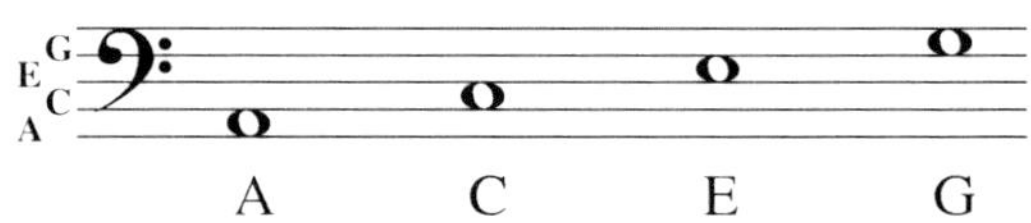

6.9 Two **often-used phrases** to remember the names of the bass clef spaces, from lowest to highest, are: **All Cows Eat Grass,** and **All Cars Eat Gas.**

☛ ***Memorize both of them!***

Middle C

6.10 Middle C is a very important note, it but doesn't have a staff line of its own. It is the note on the *first ledger line below the treble staff,* and the note on the *first ledger line above the bass staff.*

Treble Clef Middle C

Bass Clef Middle C

The Inner ACEs

6.11 It's helpful to learn that the **most-used ledger lines between the two staves** involve the word **ACE.** They are nick-named the **inner ACEs.**

6.12 The **inner ACE for the treble clef** uses *two ledger lines plus the bottom line of the treble staff* to spell **ACE:**

Treble Clef Inner ACEs

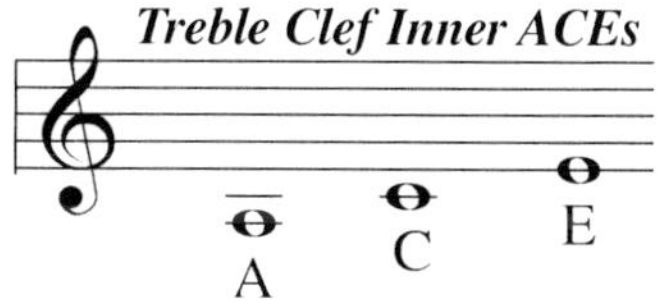

6.13 The **inner ACE for the bass clef** uses the *top line of the base staff plus two ledger lines* to spell **ACE:**

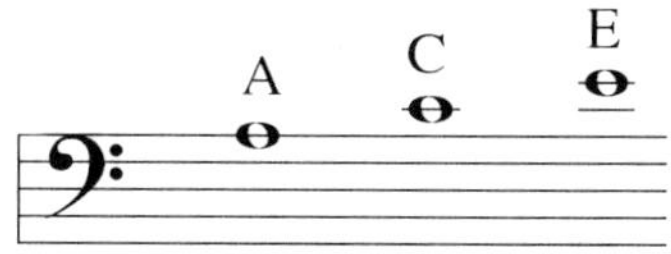

Bass Clef Inner ACEs

The Outer ACEs

6.14 It's helpful to learn that the **most-used ledger lines outside of the two staves** also involve the word **ACE.** They are nick-named the **outer ACEs.**

6.15 The **outer ACEs for the treble clef** use three ledger lines. They are the first three ledger lines *above* the treble staff:

Treble Clef Outer ACEs

6.16 The **outer ACEs for the bass clef** also use three ledger lines. They are the first three ledger lines *below* the bass staff:

Bass Clef Outer ACEs

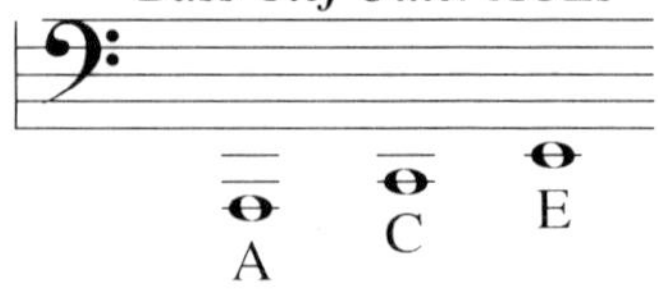

Chapter 6 Review:

After studying this lesson you should know:

1. The definition of the term *note.*
2. The seven basic note names.
3. The names of the treble-clef lines, from lowest to highest.
4. Two phrases often used to remember the names of the treble-clef lines. Memorize them!
5. The names of the treble clef spaces, from lowest to highest, and the word they spell.
6. The names of the bass-clef lines, from lowest to highest.
7. Two phrases often used to remember the names of the bass-clef lines. Memorize them!
8. The names of the bass-clef spaces, from lowest to highest.
9. Two phrases often used to remember the bass-clef spaces. Memorize them!
10. How middle C is placed on a ledger line below the treble staff and above the bass staff.
11. How to recognize the treble and bass staff inner ACEs.
12. How to recognize the treble and bass staff outer ACEs.

7

Dynamics, and Basic Musical Styles

Definitions: Dynamics, Volume, Loudness, Decibels, Dynamic Markings

7.1 The term **dynamics,** when used in the musical sense, refers to *levels of loudness,* and to *variations of contrast* in the volume, force and intensity of a musical composition.

7.2 The term **volume,** when used in the musical sense, refers to the *degree of loudness* or intensity of a sound. **Loudness** refers to the *magnitude of an auditory sensation,* which depends on the amplitude of the sound wave involved.

7.3 Loudness is measured scientifically by a machine called a **decibel meter.** A **decibel** is a *mathematical unit* for expressing how loud something is. (In more scientific terms, it is a unit for expressing the ratio of two amounts of electric or acoustic signal power equal to 10 times the common logarithm of this ratio.)

7.4 **Dynamic markings** are *written indications of the composer's desires* concerning the loudness or softness of various sections of his composition. They are usually placed just above each staff in a choral score, or above the top staff in a braced piano score.

Eight Volume-level Terms

7.5 **Eight Italian symbols or words** are used to indicate the relative loudness or softness of a musical performance. The chart below shows these symbols, the Italian terms, and the English translation of those terms.

☛ ***Memorize them in order, from softest to loudest.***

Sign	*Italian Name*	*English Meaning*
ppp	***Pianississimo***	As softly as possible
pp	***Pianissimo***	Very softly
p	***Piano***	Softly
mp	***Mezzo-Piano***	Moderately softly
mf	***Mezzo-Forte***	Moderately loudly
f	***Forte***	Loudly
ff	***Fortissimo***	Very Loudly
fff	***Fortississimo***	As loudly as possible

7.6 Two of the above symbols and Italian words include the word **mezzo.** This word means "*medium,*" "*moderately,*" or "*half.*" The English pronunciation of the word is *met-so,* with the accent on the first syllable.

Signs and Terms for Sudden Accents

7.7 Sudden accents or **changes in dynamics on a single note** are indicated by two symbols and their corresponding Italian names. These symbols are written above the staffs, just above the notes or chords to which they apply. They are:

fp	***Fortepiano***	A sudden change from loud to soft on a single note or chord
sfz	*Sforzando*	A very strong accent on a single note or chord

Signs and Terms which Request Gradual Increasing or Decreasing of Volume

7.8 Two symbols and Italian terms refer to **gradual changes of dynamics.** They are:

 ***Crescendo*** Gradually growing louder

 ***Decrescendo*** Gradually growing softer

Crescendo and Decrescendo symbols often extend over all the notes contained in several measures. They are written above or below the staffs (or between the staffs in piano music) where the gradual changes are to occur.

Basic Musical Performance Styles

7.9 There are a **variety of musical performance styles.** Competent directors clearly distinguish between these styles, and they often develop unique hand movements which convey the stylistic differences they are seeking to elicit from their performers. *Four of the most common* musical performance styles are listed and explained below.

☛ ***Memorize the four musical performance styles!***

7.10 **Legato style** means to perform notes marked *legato* in a *very smooth and connected manner.* The Italian word *legato* means *smooth.* The word ***Legato*** is written above the staffs to indicate that the style is to be used. *Legato style is an intense, very emotional style.*

A. Legato style also is indicated in music by the use of **phrase marks,** which may extend over several measures:

B. Sometimes a **tenuto mark** is placed over a note, which indicates that the note is to be *sustained for its full length.* Tenuto marks are **short dashes placed above the notes.**

7.11 Staccato style means to perform notes marked *staccato* in a *separated, detached manner,* with a period of silence between each note which is roughly equal to half of the length of the note. For example, a staccato quarter note would be performed as if it were an eighth note followed by an eighth rest. *Staccato style is a light, carefree, happy style.*

A. Staccato style is **indicated by a dot** placed above or below each note:

B. A **semi-staccato style is** sometimes requested by the conductor, in which case the notes are held longer but still separated by short rest. In this style the rests after staccato quarter notes would be about 1/4 of their length, i.e. as sixteenth rests.

7.12 Marcato style means to perform the notes in a *distinctly accented, separated, "punched" manner.* Marcato style is indicated by the word ***Marcato*** being written above the staffs where the style is to begin. *This is a forceful, dramatic, militaristic style.*

A. Marcato style often is indicated for a few particular notes by **horizontal accent marks** being placed above or below the notes:

B. **Vertical accent marks** placed above a few particular notes indicate an *even stronger accent,* such as a *sforzando,* is to be used:

C. A **semi-marcato style** is sometimes requested by the conductor, which calls for a lighter accent on the notes and shorter separations between them.

7.13 Rubato style means to perform the notes of musical phrases in a *fluctuating, uneven style as indicated by the director. Rubato* means "robbed." The word ***Rubato*** is written above the staffs where passages begin in which the style is to be used.

A. In rubato style, part of the time from a measure or phrase is ***robbed*** *from some notes and* ***given*** *to other notes* which are held longer than they would be if the phrase were directed in a strict rhythmic style.

B. **Rubato style** is *used in passages which are highly emotional,* or where the music is being adapted to the weight, sound or meaning of key words. Sometimes used to *adapt singing so it will sound more like speech,* it is often taught by conductors who have their performers mimic their spoken phrases.

Chapter 7 Review

After studying this chapter you should know:

1. The definitions of the terms: *dynamics, volume, loudness, decibel, decibel meter, dynamic markings, mezzo, pianississimo, pianissimo, piano, mezzo-piano, mezzo-forte, forte, fortissimo, fortississimo, fortepiano, sforzando, crescendo, decrescendo, phrase, tenuto, legato, staccato, marcato,* and *rubato.*
2. The signs for the eight volume-level terms, the two sudden accents terms, and the signs for gradually increasing or decreasing volume.
3. How to recognize a phrase mark, a tenuto mark, a staccato mark, a marcato mark, and an extra-strong marcato mark.
4. Know the eight volume levels in order, from softest to loudest. Memorize them!
5. Know the four basic musical performance styles. Memorize them!
6. Know how each of the four basic musical styles are indicated on musical scores, and learn your conductor's unique hand motions which are used to convey each of the styles.

8

The Keyboard, Sharps, Flats, and Accidentals

Note Names on the Piano Keyboard

8.1 A piano keyboard has **white keys** and **black keys.** The **white keys** are called **natural notes.** They are named after the first seven letters of the alphabet:

8.2 The **black keys** are called **sharp notes,** or **sharps.** Those same black keys are called **flat notes,** or **flats.**

8.3 A **sharp note** is **higher than the natural note** with the same letter name. The sharp note above **A** is called **A sharp** [written A♯]. It is the note between **A** and **B**. Other sharps on the piano keyboard are:

Name	*Written*	*Location*
C sharp	**C♯**	between **C** and **D**
D sharp	**D♯**	between **D** and **E**
F sharp	**F♯**	between **F** and **G**
G sharp	**G♯**	between **G** and **A**

8.4 A **flat note** is **lower** than the natural note with the same letter name. The flat note below B is called **B flat** [written B♭]. It is the note between **B** and **A**. Other flats on the piano keyboard are:

A flat	**A♭**	between **A** and **G**
G flat	**G♭**	between **G** and **F**
E flat	**E♭**	between **E** and **D**
D flat	**D♭**	between **D** and **C**

8.5 On the piano keyboard, there are **no black-note sharps or flats** between **B and C** nor between **E and F.**

8.6 **Enharmonic notes** are notes which are **written differently** but **sound the same.** The following are enharmonic notes:

A♯	and	**B♭**
C♯	and	**D♭**
D♯	and	**E♭**
F♯	and	**G♭**
G♯	and	**A♭**

Half-steps and Whole-steps

8.7 A **half-step** is the *distance from any note to the* ***next*** *note higher or lower.* It is the smallest distance from one note to another in written music. On the piano keyboard, the next note higher, whether a white key or a black key, is a half tone higher. A half-step is also called a *semitone.*

8.8 A **whole-step** is the distance of **two half steps** from any note, either higher or lower. It *skips over the very next note to the second-nearest note.* A whole step is also called a *tone.*

Accidentals

8.9 An **accidental** is an alteration of the pitch of one of the seven normal tones of the musical scale.

8.10 There are **five types of accidentals.** They all are written to the left of the notes they alter.

Sharps, Flats, and Naturals

8.11 A **sharp** notation *raises a note's pitch by one-half step.* An F that has been sharped is called **F sharp.** There can be a sharp on any of the seven basic notes of the musical scale. These examples show an F sharp on both the treble staff and the bass staff.

8.12 A **flat** notation lowers a *note's pitch by one-half step.* An E that has been flatted is called **E flat.** There can be a flat on any of the seven basic notes of the musical scale. These examples show an E flat on both the treble staff and the bass staff.

8.13 A **double sharp** notation *raises a note's pitch by two half steps.* This notation is made necessary when the note to be raised is already a sharped note. In most situations, the result of a double sharp is to make the note sound a full step higher. This example shows a **G double-sharp.** A G that has been double-sharped would sound the same as A.

8.14 A **double flat** notation *lowers a note's pitch by two half steps.* This notation is made necessary when the note to be lowered is already a flatted note. In most situations, the result of a double flat is to make the note sound a full step below. This example shows an **A double-flat.** An A that has been double-flatted would sound the same as G.

8.15 A **natural** notation *cancels a previous accidental* (a sharp, flat, double sharp, or double flat), whether it has *previously occurred in the measure* or whether it is *in the key signature.* This is a natural sign, placed to the left of the note it is intended to alter.

Key Signatures and Accidentals in Measures

8.16 Sharps or flats occurring in key signatures remain in effect *until the end of the piece,* or until the *next key change.*

8.17 Accidentals that occur in a measure affect their designated notes *for that measure only.* Their effect ends at the next bar line.

Chapter 8 Review

After studying this lesson you should know:

1. The definitions of the following terms: *sharps, flats, enharmonic notes, half step, whole step, accidental, double sharp, double flat,* and *natural.*
2. The names of the white and black notes on the piano keyboard.
3. The five black-note sharps on the piano keyboard.
4. The five black-note flats on the piano keyboard.
5. The five types of accidentals.
6. How sharps or flats in a key signature differ from accidentals in specific measures.

9

Special Music Markings, a Pitch-locating System

Dotted Notes

9.1 A **dot placed after a note** makes the note last *one-and-a-half times its normal length.*

A. A half note (𝅗𝅥) lasts for two beats. A **dotted half note** (𝅗𝅥.) lasts for three beats.

B. A quarter note (♩) lasts for one beat. A **dotted quarter note** (♩.) lasts for one-and-a-half notes.

C. An eighth note (♪) lasts for one-half a beat. A **dotted eighth note** (♪.) lasts for 3/4 of a beat, and often is *paired with a sixteenth note* (♪. 𝅘𝅥𝅯).

9.2 Very occasionally, **two dots are placed after a note.** *Each dot adds half as much as the previous dot.*

𝅗𝅥.. = 𝅗𝅥 + ♩ + ♪

9.3 **Dots can be placed after rests** and work the same way.

Ties and Slurs

9.4 A **tie** is *a curved line used to join two notes* to extend the length of time the first note is held. Notes can only be tied when they are **exactly the same note** [two Cs, etc.]. When two notes are tied together, *the second note is not sounded,* but the first note is *held for the combined time value of the two notes.* Ties are often used to extend a note over a bar line into the next measure. *A tie is a rhythm marker.*

This note receives 7 counts.

9.5 A **slur** is a curved line over several **different notes.** It means to perform the notes in a *smooth* and *connected* manner. *A slur is a performance-style marker.*

9.6 A **slur over two notes** is an instruction to *release the second note gently:*

9.7 Slurs are used to show how **groups of words or notes are to be connected together.** They are often used to tell singers *where not to breathe.* Slurs also are used to indicate "bowing" patterns for stringed instruments.

Triplets

9.8 Sometimes **three notes are fitted into the time of two notes,** *squeezing three beats into two counts.* The three notes are grouped together by a curved line and the figure *3*. When performing **triplets,** each note of the triplet should be given the same length as the others.

Quarter-note triplets ***Eighth-note triplets***

8va Octave Marks

9.9 The abbreviation **8va, followed by a dashed line,** indicates that the notes over which it is placed are to be *performed an octave higher until the end of the dashed line is reached.* An 8va can also be placed *under* notes, meaning that they are *to be played an octave lower.*

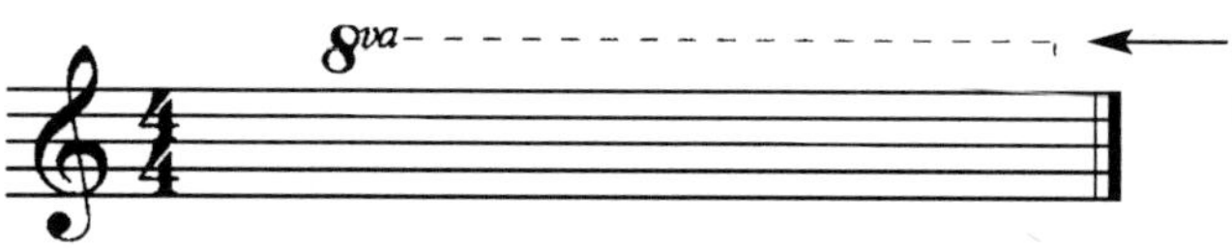

Notes under this mark are played 8 notes higher than written.

Counting Measures with Pickup Notes

9.10 When the **notes in the beginning measure** of a piece use fewer than the number of beats per measure indicated in the time signature, the *notes in the incomplete measure are called* **pickup notes.**

Pickup notes, starting on beat 3.

9.11 When the **first measure of a piece is incomplete** because it contains pickup notes, *the unused beats from the first measure will be placed in the* **last measure of the piece,** which will also have an *incomplete number of beats.*

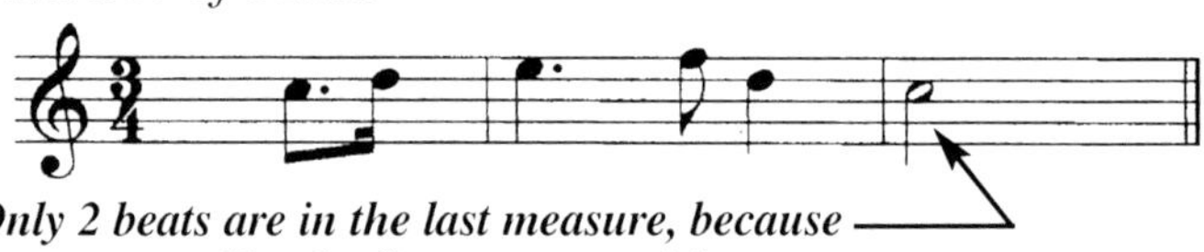

Only 2 beats are in the last measure, because 1 beat was used by the first measure pickup notes.

9.12 To determine what beat pickup notes begin on, count backward *from the first bar line that follows them, the number of beats they use,* and then *subtract that number from the total number of beats in the measure.* This will indicate the number of unused beats which precede the pickup notes. *Then subtract that number from the total number of beats in the measure to know on what beat-number the pickup notes begin.* [For example, in a piece with a 3/4 time signature, there is one quarter-note pickup. Three beats minus one beat equals two unused beats, so the pickup begins on the third beat of the measure, and there will be only two beats in the last measure of the piece.]

A Pitch–locating System

9.13 A **sometimes-used octave-classification system** has been devised so pitches can be easily defined and communicated to others.

A. In this system, the ascending octave beginning two Cs below Middle C is called the **great octave.** Notes in that octave are written in capital letters (C), or verbally described as "*great C, great D,*" etc.

B. The next octave up is called the **small octave.** Notes in this octave are written in lower-case letters (c), and are verbally described as "*small c, small d,*" etc.

C. The next octave up, which *begins with Middle C,* is called the **1 octave.** Notes in this octave are *written in lower-case letters followed with a super-script [raised] number* 1, or are verbally described as "c^1, d^1, e^1," etc.

D. The next three octaves up are described as the **2,** or **3,** or **4 octaves,** and are written and verbally expressed in the same manner as in item C, above.

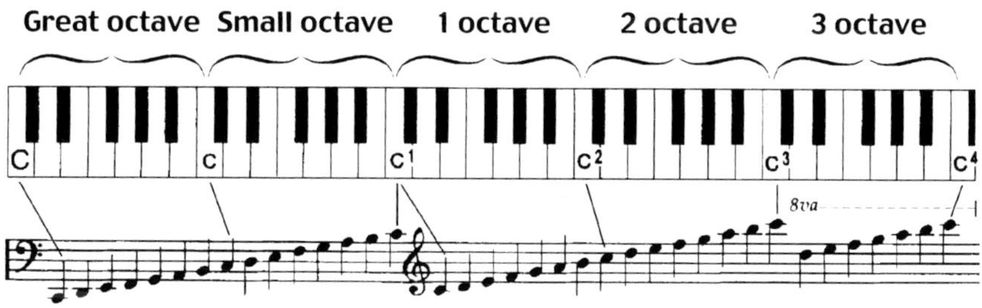

Chapter 9 Review

After studying this chapter you should know:

1. The definitions of the following terms: *dotted note, double-dotted note, tie, slur, triplet, 8va,* and *pickup note.*
2. How dots placed after notes, and also ties, influence notes' time values.
3. What slurs indicate and how notes marked with slurs should be performed.
4. How triplets are identified and performed.
5. How notes marked 8va are performed.
6. How pickup notes affect the number of beats in the first and last measures of a piece, and how to determine on what beat the pickup notes begin.
7. How to write and verbally express note names using the pitch-locating system.

10

The Major Scale Pattern, Intervals, and Triads

Definitions: Interval, Prime, Octave, Chromatic Scale

10.1 An **interval** is the *pitch difference* between two degrees of the scale. An interval usually is measured from the lower of any two pitches. As will be seen, the number of degrees which separate the two notes determines the interval and its name.

10.2 The term **prime** is applied to the lower of two pitches when an interval is being measured. Prime means *base, first,* or *original.* In music, it also means **unison,** meaning two notes which have the same pitch. Any note can be a prime.

10.3 An **octave** is a note which has the same name as another note, but is eight notes higher or lower. For example, an A to the next higher or lower A; a C to the next higher or lower C.

The top notes are an octave above the corresponding notes beneath them.

Chromatic Scales

10.4 A **chromatic scale** is a scale that *moves up or down by half steps.*

A. A chromatic scale can be **written in sharps** and is usually written in sharps when it is an *ascending scale:*

B. A chromatic scale can also be **written in flats,** and is usually written in flats when it is a *descending scale:*

Notice that sharps and flats are **placed *before* the notes** on the staff (♯♩), but ***after* the letter name** of the note when it is written as a word (C♯).

The Major Scale Pattern

10.5 A **half step** is the smallest interval in the chromatic scale. It is the distance between a prime and the note closest to it. The distance between C and C-sharp is a half step.

10.6 A **whole step** is an interval of two half steps. It is the distance between a prime and the note just beyond the note closest to it. The distance between C and D is a whole step.

10.7 A **major scale** is made up of a combination of five whole steps and two half steps. It has whole steps between all the notes except half steps between the 3rd and 4th notes and the 7th and 8th notes.

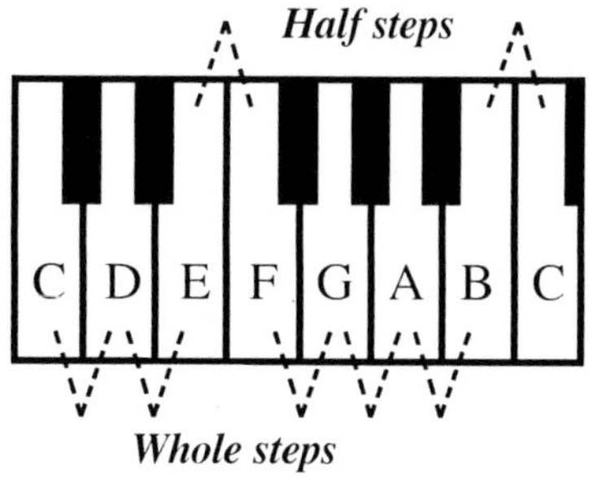

10.8 The **major scale pattern** is the same as is found on a piano keyboard **for octaves beginning and ending with C.** This pattern is sometimes expressed in this list:

Whole step	**C** to **D**
Whole step	**D** to **E**
Half step	**E** to **F**
Whole step	**F** to **G**
Whole step	**G** to **A**
Whole step	**A** to **B**
Half step	**B** to **C**

Intervals

10.9 The intervals in the Major Scale Pattern are:

	Name	*Consists of*
	**Major 2nd**	One whole step
	**Major 3rd**	Two whole steps
	**Perfect 4th**	Two whole steps and a half step
	**Perfect 5th**	Three whole steps and a half step
	**Major 6th**	Four whole steps and a half step
	**Major 7th**	Five whole steps and a half step
	**Perfect 8th Octave**	Five whole steps and two half steps

10.10 Minor intervals can be *created by lowering the top note of any of the four major intervals by a half step.* The intervals that can be altered this way are **Major 2nds, Major 3rds, Major 6ths** and **Major 7ths.** These are the minor intervals:

	Name	*Consists of*
	**Minor 2nd**	One half step
	**Minor 3rd**	One whole step and one half step
	**Minor 6th**	Four whole steps
	**Minor 7th**	Five whole steps

10.11 Augmented intervals are perfect intervals that have been *made larger by raising the top note a half step:*

	**Augmented 4th**	Three whole steps (This is also a **Diminished 5th.**)
	**Augmented 5th**	Four whole steps (This is also a **Minor 6th.**)

10.12 Diminished intervals are perfect intervals that have been *made smaller by lowering the top note a half step:*

	**Diminished 5th**	Three whole steps

A Diminished 4th is actually a Major 3rd, so it is only rarely used.

10.13 Intervals are called **harmonic intervals** when two tones are *sounded together:*

10.14 Intervals are called **melodic intervals** if two tones are *not sounded at the same time* but are consecutive tones of a melodic line:

Triads

10.15 A **chord** is produced when *three or more notes are sounded together.*

10.16 **Triads** are *three-part chords.* Often, one of the three notes is doubled to produce four-part harmony.

10.17 There are two basic kinds of triads: **major triads** and **minor triads.**

A. This is a **major triad.** It has a *major third* on the *bottom* and a *minor third* on the top:

B. This is a **minor triad.** It has a *minor third* on the *bottom* and a *major third* on the *top:*

10.18 **Triads** can be *made on every note of the scale.* The triads built on the seven natural tones are:

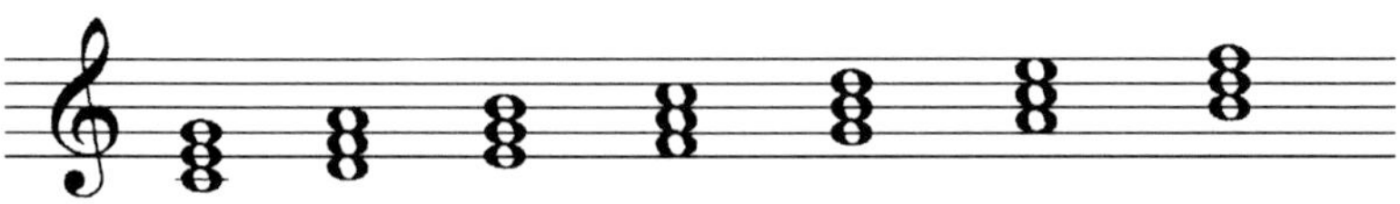

A. The scale degrees of the above triads are usually **labeled in Roman numerals** from one to seven [I-vii].

B. Those that are **major triads** (with a *major third* on the *bottom* and a *minor third* on the *top*) are shown with **capital letters** beneath them (I, IV, V).

C. Those that are **minor triads** (with a *minor third* on the *bottom* and a *major third* on the *top*) are shown in **lower-case letters** (ii, iii, vi).

D. The triad on the seventh degree of the scale is a **diminished triad** because it consists of *two minor triads.* It is written with a small raised circle to the right of its letter name (vii°) to show that it is a diminished triad.

Chapter 10 Review

After studying this chapter you should:

1. Know the definitions of the terms: *interval, prime, unison, octave, chromatic scale, half step, whole step, major scale, major, minor, augmented, diminished, harmonic interval, melodic interval, chord,* and *triad.*
2. Be able to recognize and name all the notes in a chromatic scale, using both sharps and flats, written on either the treble or the bass staff.
3. Know when and why chromatic scales are written in sharps, and when and why they are written in flats.
4. Know and be able to explain the major scale pattern, demonstrating where the whole steps and half steps occur.
5. Know and recognize all the intervals in a major scale pattern. Know which are major intervals and which are perfect intervals, and know how many whole and half steps they each contain.
6. Know and recognize minor intervals. Know how they relate to the major intervals in the major scale pattern.
7. Know and recognize augmented and diminished intervals. Know how they relate to the perfect intervals in the major scale pattern.
8. Know and recognize major and minor triads and be able to explain how they differ from each other.

11

Scales, Keys, and Key Signatures

Scales

11.1 A **scale** is a *series of notes in alphabetical order* starting with the key note after which the scale is named.

11.2 A **tonality** is an *organized relationship of musical tones.* It is based on a central tone which all the other notes support or tend toward in one way or another. Tonality is *a synonym for the word* **key.**

11.3 A **key note** is the starting note of a scale, and that *scale follows the whole-step and half-step plan* which constitutes a **key.** It is the *note for which the scale is named,* and is the *first note of that scale.* The key note is the *main tone,* or "*home base*" of the scale. All the other tones of the scale support it or lean toward it. Most compositions end on a chord built on the key note, called a **tonic chord.**

Major Keys

11.4 Major keys, and their scales, have a **pattern of whole steps and half steps.** As has been seen, that pattern is:

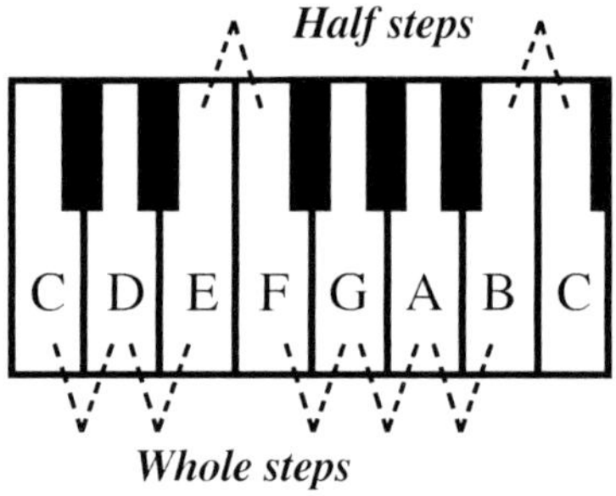

Major keys have a *bright, happy sound.*

11.5 **Major keys** can be *built on any note.* They are structured through the use of sharps or flats in their key signatures so the major-key pattern of whole steps and half steps is maintained. There are **15 major keys.**

A. The **key of C has no sharps or flats.**

B. There are **seven keys that have sharps** in their key signatures. They are **G** (1 sharp), **D** (2 sharps), **A** (3 sharps), **E** (4 sharps), **B** (5 sharps), **F♯** (6 sharps), and **C♯** (7 sharps).

C. There are **seven keys that have flats** in their key signatures. They are **F** (1 flat), **B♭** (2 flats), **E♭** (3 flats) **A♭** (4 flats), **D♭** (5 flats), **G♭** (6 flats), and **C♭** (7 flats).

D. **Three** of the sharp keys are **enharmonic** with three of the flat keys (meaning that they sound the same but are written differently). The key of **B** (5 sharps) sounds the same as the key of **C♭** (7 flats). The key of **F♯** (6 sharps) sounds the same as the key of **G♭** (6 flats). The key of **C♯** (7 sharps) sounds the same as the key of **D♭** (5 flats).

11.6 The **circle of fifths** is an interesting pattern that occurs in the names of the musical keys.

A. When **one more sharp is added** to the previous key, the *new key is a perfect fifth* ***above*** *the previous key.*

B. When **one more flat is added** to the previous key, the *new key is a perfect fifth* ***below*** *the previous key.*

C. This is a **chart** of **the circle of fifths:**

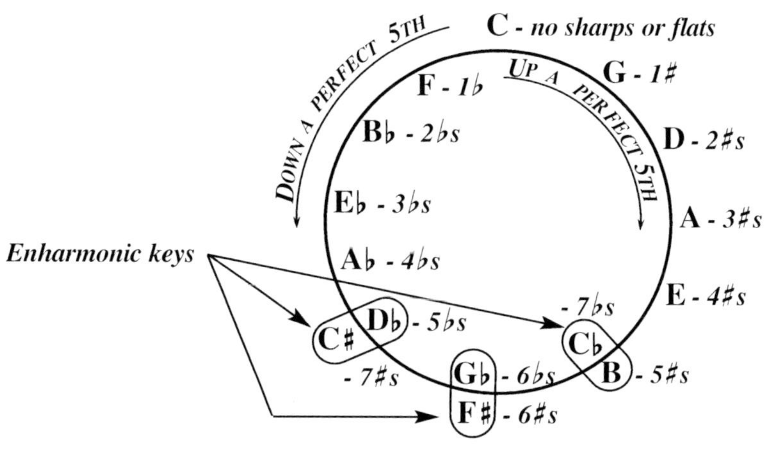

The Natural Minor Scale

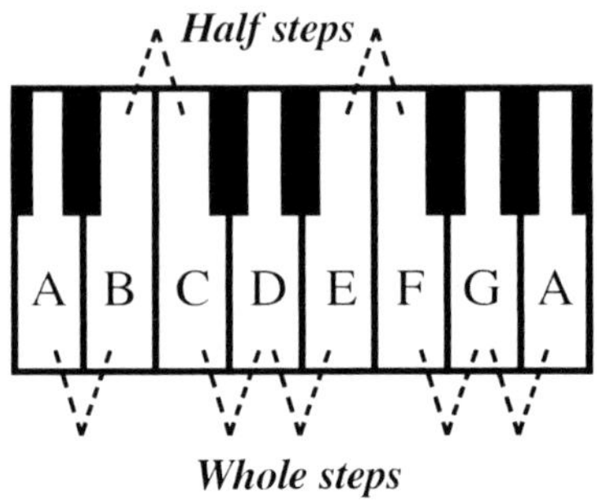

11.7 **Minor keys,** like major keys, have a pattern of whole steps and half steps. Actually, there are several minor key patterns. This pattern is the **natural minor** key pattern:

Minor keys have a serious, somber, sad sound.

11.8 Like major keys, minor keys can be built on any note, so there are also **15 minor key signatures.**

A. To make their whole-step half-step patterns match the sharps and flats in the various major key signatures, the **minor scales start three notes lower** (*a minor 3rd lower, meaning a whole step plus a half step lower*) than the major scales with the same sharps or flats in their key signatures.

B. These minor keys and scales which start a minor 3rd lower than their major scale signatures are called **relative minor** scales and keys.

The Harmonic Minor and Melodic Minor Scales

11.9 Another minor scale pattern, the **harmonic minor,** follows the same pattern as the natural minor pattern except that *the seventh note is raised a half step.* This note is raised through the use of **accidentals** which occur in the various measures rather than in the key signature.

11.10 A third minor scale pattern is the **melodic minor.** It follows the same pattern as the natural minor pattern except that *the sixth and seventh notes are both raised a half step.* This is done through the use of accidentals which occur in the various measures rather than in the key signatures.

11.11 **Sharps** are *always printed in the same order* in a key signature, and *previous sharps must all be present* when new sharps are added. Note the **layout pattern:** three rows, with *two* sharps in the first row, *three* in the second row, and *two* in the third row. *Each sharp is a perfect fifth up from its predecessor.*

11.12 **Flats** are *always printed in the same order* in a key signature, and *previous flats must all be present* when new flats are added. Note the **layout pattern:** *three rows of two flats,* plus an *extra flat.* Note how *both rows descend stepwise.* Each flat is a perfect fourth from its predecessor. (Note that **up a fourth is equal to down a fifth,** except for an octave's difference.)

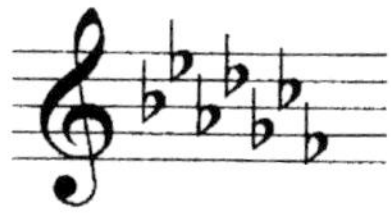

Major and Relative Minor Key Signatures and Scales

11.13 The following chart shows each of the 15 major keys, their relative minor keys, and their key signatures.

Major Key	*Relative Minor Key*	*Key Signature*
	No Sharps or Flats	
C Major	**A Minor**	No Sharps or Flats
	Sharp Keys	
G Major	**E Minor**	1 Sharp
D Major	**B Minor**	2 Sharps
A Major	**F♯ Minor**	3 Sharps
E Major	**C♯ Minor**	4 Sharps
B Major	**G♯ Minor**	5 Sharps
F♯ Major	**D♯ Minor**	6 Sharps
C♯ Major	**A♯ Minor**	7 Sharps
	Flat Keys	
F Major	**D Minor**	1 Flat
B♭ Major	**G Minor**	2 Flats

Flat Keys (continued)

E♭ Major	**C Minor**	3 Flats
A♭ Major	**F Minor**	4 Flats
D♭ Major	**B♭ Minor**	5 Flats
G♭ Major	**E♭ Minor**	6 Flats
C♭ Major	**A♭ Minor**	7 Flats

Rules for Identifying Major Key Names

☛ *Memorize the following rules:*

11.14 The rule for identifying the names of major sharp keys is: ***The name of a major key with sharps in its key signature is the name of the note which is a half-step above the name of the last sharp in the key signature.***

11.15 The rule for identifying the names of major flat keys is: ***The name of a major key with flats in its key signature is the name of the next-to-the-last flat in the key signature.*** Memorize that a key signature with one flat is the key of F.

Chapter 11 Review

After studying this lesson you should know:

1. The definition of the following terms: *scale, tonality, key, key note, tonic chord, major key, circle of fifths, relative minor keys, natural minor key, harmonic minor key,* and *melodic minor key.*
2. The whole-step pattern for major keys, natural minor keys, harmonic minor keys, and melodic minor keys.
3. How to explain the relationship between a major key and its relative minor key, what change is made to create a harmonic minor key, and what changes are made to create a melodic minor key.
4. The names of the seven sharps in their order, and the names of the seven flats in their order.
5. The rules for identifying the names of major sharp and flat keys from their key signatures.

Index